Financial Assistance

for Artists

Financial Assistance for Artists

Edition 1

Jason T. Uhl

Financial Assistance for Artists

Financial Assistance for Artists

Grants, Fellowships, Publishers, Galleries, and Basic Business Practices for Artists

by Jason Uhl

Disclaimer

This compilation of opportunities does not guarantee any specific amount of monetary support or other support to any individual. All opportunities must be applied for and acceptance and promise of any monetary amount is at the discretion of the foundation or organization providing such opportunities. This book is meant to be an artist's resource and compilation of various opportunities that you may or may not be eligible for. This book is a one of a kind compilation meant to bring various opportunities largely unknown to artists to their attention. This book is the result of years of online research into available artist opportunities resultant from publicly available information available on the internet.

--This book is dedicated to all artists, struggling and successful, may the information contained in this volume help you on your journey and help you become the artist you strive to be.

Table of Contents

A Brief Introduction from the Author

Starving artist no more! With this compendium of information compiled from years of research of publicly available online information you no longer have to suffer because you want to pursue your artistic dreams. Every year thousands and thousands of artists seek funding assistance from local and state art counsels so that they may continue to pursue their artistic dreams and passions. A relatively unknown source of funding to artists today is private foundations and organizations that provide monetary support only to individual artists. The problem with seeking funding from many local and state art counsels is that they are required by the state or by their regulations to only provide monetary support to artists for projects that directly involve the community. Community based art projects play a very important role in our communities; these projects are wonderful events that bring culture and vibrance into our communities all across the United States. The problem with many local and state counsels is that they are of little assistance to the individual artist seeking to improve his or her own art form. Artists looking to concentrate on their own personal work, to improve their skills, and looking to explore new areas of art, unless they have the monetary means to support their endeavors, many times find themselves giving up on their dreams. It is at this point that the individual artist can take advantage of many relatively unknown monetary support services, namely, private foundations and organizations. After a simple application process artists' everyday find that they can pursue their dreams and their passions because of the assistance they have received from these private foundations and other organizations.

The business of fine art can be very lucrative, competitive, stressful, and challenging, but to the same extent very rewarding. Knowing that your work will be appreciated and cherished by others for years, and hopefully generations to come makes all your hard work seem very valid and very worthwhile. You have to assume the responsibility of sales person, marketer, and artist in this profession, and to survive you have to complete these tasks well. In order to succeed in your art you only have to be satisfied with the art you produce. In order to succeed financially with your art you have to try to out perform every other artist around you. This is a daunting task, marketing and sales will usually consume more of your time than you actually get to spend on creating art. In this volume you will find information on basic business practices, national and international grants and fellowships, grants and fellowships for each of the geographical areas of the United States (East, Midwest, West), residency programs in the Unites States and abroad, art and craft galleries and retailers located in the United States, art book publishers, and print and poster publishers. I have compiled the information in this book from the vast amount of publicly available information available on the internet in an effort to help you get your art business started or to help you pursue your artistic dreams and desires. With some general information on business practices of artists and where you may find funding that may help further your artistic career and artistic endeavors you can realize your dreams.

Best Wishes

-- Jason Uhl

Chapter 1

Getting Your Art Business Started

The business of fine art can be very lucrative, competitive, stressful, and challenging, but to the same extent very rewarding. Knowing that your work will be appreciated and cherished by others for years, and hopefully generations to come can make all your hard work seem very valid and worthwhile. One of the most important things we must remember as artisans is that we must also accept the role of salesman; it is part of the business of being an artist. Like any good salesman you must know your product and you should be able to promote your product successfully. When your art is your product, and you reach a level of successful promotion, you must then be ready and prepared to close the sales that happen to come your way. Unfortunately, the independent artist is not supplied with all of the business forms and legal documents one would readily find and have access to in other sales atmospheres. The creation and successful use of these documents in your business is one of your main responsibilities, in addition to being the great artist that you are. The bill of sale or receipt, terms and conditions of sale including return and defect policies, credit/debit card processing, and certificates of authenticity are some of the key topics and documents you will need to utilize to successfully sell your art and keep your patrons satisfied and coming back for more of your work.

As artists, we are solely accountable for making sure that consumers and patrons of our work completely understand the terms of which we are conducting our business under. If you plan on personally selling your arts and/or crafts from your own shop or studio, you should develop a personalized sales form or receipt or have one created for you. Many prefer using their own personal receipt forms rather than using a basic and many times bland cash register slip only. For those who cannot afford a cash register or do not feel one would be appropriate for there business setting, I strongly recommend using a personalized receipt form. These receipt forms can be simply printed off your home computer on personal stationary or any other paper and can add a little extra flare to your business documentation. This form should clearly explain in black and white what the customer is receiving. Your receipt form should include your complete contact information, the date of the purchase, a clear description of the item being sold including mediums, formats, and/or dimensions. Is your customer purchasing an original piece of art, a reproduction print, an item of limited edition, a signed item, etc., and what condition is this piece of art in? This form should also contain the standard subtotal, sales tax, and total blanks, and may include a section for any fees, shipping and handling charges, or other miscellaneous fees that may be associated with the purchase of your art. You may also be interested in adding a detachable section on your sale slip to record the purchasers contact information. This can become a good way to begin to develop a mailing list if you were to publish a newsletter or wanted to send postcards or invites for an open house, a special sale, or for a customer discount. A personalized, but still basic sales receipt form will ease the pressure of closing your sale successfully. The more personalized the experience with your customer the more likely they will be to remember you and your art work in the future. Creating a lasting impact on current and prospective customers is a key lesson to be learned. Customers don't like to be confused, so don't confuse them with a jumbled or haphazard looking receipt after their purchase, and don't confuse them with a complicated return or exchange policy. Impress them with a personalized, professional looking, clear, and concise receipt.

Be creative, be bold, and make all your business forms stand out. I also strongly recommend printing the terms and/or the conditions of sale on the back of any receipt so as to not over-clutter the front-design of the receipt. Your receipt form should also include an area that specifies whether the purchase is being made by cash, check, credit, or debit card. Most credit companies will have a merchant division or merchant contacts from which you may obtain a credit card swiper. I recommend contacting Retriever/First of Omaha Merchant Processing at 1-888-549-6424. They have no application fee, have no monthly minimums, and have no lease requirements for their credit/debit processing equipment. I strongly suggest obtaining credit/debit processing equipment, an ever increasing amount of sales worldwide are completed through credit and debit card transactions.

The terms and conditions of sale are integral parts of receipts, and will ultimately affect the entire selling process. Terms and conditions also usually explain in detail any type of guarantee offered by the artist in lue of a possible merchandise defect. Your terms and conditions of sale can be as strict or as lenient as you want to make them. You may choose to accept the return of any piece of your art at any time; you may set a time limit on returns, 30, 60, 90 days, etc. You may choose to charge a re-stocking fee on returned items. I strongly recommend developing at least a basic return and guarantee against defect policy. This ensures safeguards against any fraudulent practices by either party. By developing very clear and concise terms and conditions of sale you will save yourself from a lot of potential headaches in the future.

A certificate of authenticity guarantees one who purchases a work of art that it is in fact a genuine piece by the artist or a limited reproduction by the artist and/or publishing company. The certificate of authenticity validates and sets apart true fine art and limited edition printings from mass production printings of open editions. When it comes down to unique fine art vs. mass production you will begin to notice a dichotomy, the personalized nature of unique fine art is a much more attractive investment to art buyers. When someone buys your art I urge you to think of them as making not only a financial investment, but also a spiritual and intellectual investment in their future, their children's future, and their community's future. Your art will in some form impact everyone who looks at it. Art appreciation in your community grows every time a customer purchases a piece of your art, therefore exposing your work, talent, and love for what you do to the rest of the community. A professional, thorough, and truthful certificate of authenticity, especially one signed by the actual artist him or herself, is an important step in developing a personal relationship with the patron of your work. This bond is made even stronger when a signed artists' statement also accompanies every piece of art that he or she sells. The certificate of authenticity's main purpose, over all others, is to be a safeguard against individuals committing art fraud. In other words the certificate is there to stop someone else from copying your work and selling the copy as an original. If all of your work is accompanied by a very thorough and signed certificate, you then greatly reduce the risk of your work being able to be successfully copied and sold as original by some one committing art fraud. What is in a certificate of authenticity? Two of the first items you should see on a certificate of authenticity are the artist's full name and the title of the artwork that is being bought. These two items are absolutely necessary, the following remaining items are also very important when establishing legitimate certificates for your art. There are no laws governing the issuance of certificates of authenticity, so it is very important to include as many of these items as possible when creating legitimate professional certificates of authenticity.

1. The artist's full signature in ink.
2. On what date was the art work produced?
3. Who was involved in the production of the art?
4. What are the exact dimensions of the piece, image size, paper size, canvas size, etc?
5. Is the artist or a publishing company issuing the certificate?
6. What medium or special technique was used in the creation of this piece of art?
7. What material is this piece of art on or encased in?
>   **If this is a limited edition work, what number of the edition is it, and how many limited works were produced in total and on what date was this work created?
8. If you are creating work of a limited edition, are any of the works proofs?
9. Was this work created in a special workshop area, an artist's colony, or in your personal studio?
10. What is the address, telephone number, email, etc. of the certificate issuer and/or artist?

There is no true order that these items must be in, but they should be organized in a manner that is aesthetically pleasing to look at, very professional, thorough, and truthful.

Take slides and photographs of all of your work. I cannot stress enough the importance of taking slides or photographs of your work. You never know when an income opportunity will arise that a good slide of your work will help you to attain. It may be a competition in the arts, a magazine, book, or other publication opportunity, or to accompany materials for a collegiate application, either for educational acceptance or employment. Take slides of your work and make sure they are spectacular, sharp, clear, and detailed. The slides of your work should represent the best of your aesthetic and technical abilities as an artist. When you have organized all of your materials, have developed creative and professional looking documents, and have properly documented all of your artistic work you can approach the marketing and sales of your art in a much more confident manner.

There are six main factors you have to look at when beginning a career as an artist. First, you must decide how you as an artist will begin to promote your artwork and how you will develop your reputation. Seek locations throughout your community that you can display some of your works for free. Some of these locations may include local libraries and other public places. Many public locales are continually looking for new, innovative, and or other art works representing the local culture of the region. Secondly, you will want to speak with all of the local colleges and universities in your area. Most colleges and universities have galleries and other administrative buildings and classrooms that house many various works of art intended to create, inspire, and culture the campus community. A personal show at a local college or university can be an extremely effective way to begin to develop relations with many individuals in the art community in your area and elsewhere. Thirdly, you should send portfolios of work available to galleries, museums, and retailers of art. There will be galleries available to you and seeking new work from you both locally and nationally and internationally. You never know what type of work a gallery or museum may decide to promote next, it very well may be what you as an artist create. Fourthly, it is important to think about licensing your work for mass production. Many artists now make there soul source of income from licensing their works to print and poster publishers. Licensing your work requires sending out many portfolios of your best works, but can pay off greatly. Companies licensing art work will choose specific works they know will be the most profitable for them in the markets they sell the largest portion of product in, most companies that accept your work will license your work as either an open print or a limited edition print. Fifthly, it is important if you have the time and capacity to become involved in and have booths at local, regional, and national art shows, fairs, and expos. Having a booth at these shows greatly expands your visibility and reputation within the community in which the show is held. You can also increase exposure through submitting pieces to magazines, journals, and other print media. Sixthly, it is important to develop a website of your work and credentials, this will allow individuals world-wide to view your work 24-hours a day, order your work 24-hours a day, and communicate with you 24-hours a day. With all of the promotional materials you use to promote your artwork and at all of the promotional events and shows you attend, you should include a business card with all of your sales and inquiries and this should include your website address and other contact information. A simple business card can be a very powerful marketing tool for the artist.

Chapter 2

Finding the Funding You Need with Grants and Fellowships
(organized alphabetically)

National and International Grants and Fellowships

A ROOM OF HER OWN FOUNDATION
Writer and Artist Grants--up to $50,000.
P. O. Box 778
Placitas, NM 87043
http://www.aroomofherownfoundation.org
info@aroomofherownfoundation.org
A Room of Her Own Foundation is a non-profit organization that promotes the work of women artists (painting, photography, sculpture) and writers (fiction, non-fiction, poetry, playwriting) in communities throughout the United States.

AARON SISKIND FOUNDATION
Photographer Grants--up to $5000.
School of Visual Arts
214 E. 21st Street
New York, NY 10010
(609) 348-5650
http://www.aaronsiskind.org
info@aaronsiskind.org
The Aaron Siskind Foundation promotes artistic achievement in the field of contemporary photography (still photography, media arts).

ADOLPH AND ESTHER GOTTLIEB FOUNDATION
Emergency Artist Grants--up to $10,000
380 West Broadway
New York, NY 10012
(212) 226-0581
http://www.gottliebfoundation.org
shirsch@gottliebfoundation.org
The Adolph and Esther Gottlieb Foundation was established in an effort to assist individual visual artists, the foundation offers a support grant and an emergency grant to qualified and approved applicants.

ADOLPH AND ESTHER GOTTLIEB FOUNDATION
Advanced Career Artist Grants--up to $20,000
380 West Broadway
New York, NY 10012
(212) 226-0581
http://www.gottliebfoundation.org
shirsch@gottliebfoundation.org
The Adolph and Esther Gottlieb Foundation was established in an effort to assist individual visual artists, the foundation offers a support grant and an emergency grant to qualified and approved applicants.

AID FOR ARTISANS, INC.
Artist Group Grants--up to unknown amount
14 Brick Walk Lane
Farmington, CT. 06032
(860)-947-3344
http://www.aid2artisans.org
Aid For Artisans, Inc. is a nonprofit organization founded in order to provide economic aid in the form of grants and other assistance to individual artists and craft persons around the world.

ALDRICH MUSEUM OF CONTEMPORARY ART
Emerging Artist Grant--up to $3000
258 Main Street
Ridgefield, CT 06877
http://www.aldrichart.org
The Aldrich Museum of Contemporary Art exhibits expressive and compelling contemporary art work from emerging and mid-career artists, and strives to support individual artists in our community.

ALDRICH MUSEUM OF CONTEMPORARY ART
Larry Aldrich Grant--up to $25,000
258 Main Street
Ridgefield, CT 06877
http://www.aldrichart.org
The Aldrich Museum of Contemporary Art exhibits expressive and compelling contemporary art work from emerging and mid-career artists, and strives to support individual artists in our community.

ALEXIA FOUNDATION
Professional Alexia Grant—up to $15,000
116 Oceanport Avenue
Little Silver, NJ 07739
(315) 443-2304
http://www.alexiafoundation.org/
dcsuther@syr.edu
The Alexia Foundation is a nonprofit foundation that strives to promote world peace through support of both professional and student photographers and photo-journalists by granting economic assistance and scholarships to individuals whose work promotes world peace.

ALLIANCE FOR YOUNG ARTISTS & WRITERS
Scholastic Art & Writing Grant--up to $5000
557 Broadway
New York, NY 10012
(212) 343-6100
http://www.scholastic.com/artandwriting
A&WgeneralInfo@scholastic.com
The Scholastic Art and Writing Awards have been identifying and promoting the artistry of young visual and literary artists for over 80 years. The awards are administered by the Alliance for Young Artists and Writers, Inc., a nonprofit organization dedicated to the support of young artists.

ALLIGATOR JUNIPER
Alligator Juniper Photography Contest--up to $500
220 Grove Ave.
Prescott College
Prescott, AZ 86301
(928) 778-2090
http://www.prescott.edu/highlights/alligator_juniper/index.html
aj@prescott.edu
Alligator Juniper is a publication produced by Prescott College in Prescott, Arizona. The college awards publication and a grant to both students and individual visual artists and literary artists nationally. The magazine features fiction, non-fiction, poetry, and black and white photography.

AMERICAN CERAMIC CIRCLE, INC.
American Ceramic Circle Research Grants—up to $5000
P.O. Box 224
Williamsburg, VA 23187-0224
http://www.amercercir.org/
amercercir@aol.com
The American Ceramic Circle, Inc. is a nonprofit organization committed to the promotion of the ceramic arts. Founded in 1970, the organization provides grants to individuals for research in ceramic history.

AMERICAN INSTITUTE OF ARCHITECTS
AIA Photography Competition--up to $500
911 Washington Ave. #225
St. Louis, MO 63101-1203
(314) 621-3484
http://www.aia-stlouis.org
chapter@aia-stlouis.org
The St. Louis Chapter of the American Institute of Architects provides a photography award to winning applicants in their yearly AIA Photography Competition. Applicants must be architects or architecture students.

ART LIBRARIES SOCIETY OF NORTH AMERICA
H.W. Wilson Foundation Research Grant--up to $2000
329 March Road, Suite 232
Box 11
Kanata
Ontario K2K 2E1
Canada
(800) 817-0621
http://www.arlisna.org
arlisna@igs.net
The H.W. Wilson Foundation Research Grant program is a grant program
supported by the Art Libraries Society of North America. The award is open to
members if the society in the individual areas of librarianship, art curatorship, and
the general arts.

ARTADIA
Artist Grants--up to $15,000
210 Eleventh Avenue, Suite 503
New York, NY 10001
(212) 727-2233
http://www.artadia.org/
info@artadia.org
Artadia is a nonprofit organization based in New York and awards monetary
support to individual artists in selected cities throughout the United States.
Artadia is an organization that strives to promote the importance of art in our
communities and has built a national network of support for artisans.

ARTISTS' FELLOWSHIP
Emergency Grants--up to unknown amt.
47 Fifth Avenue
New York, NY 10003
(646) 230-9833
http://www.artistsfellowship.com/home.html
Artists' Fellowship, Inc. is a private charitable foundation that provides support to
individual professional fine artists during times of bereavement, emergency, or
disability.

ARTOUTTHERE.COM
Artist Grants--up to unknown amt.
P.O. Box 3637
Lawrence, KS 66046
(785) 841-3834
http://www.artoutthere.com
info@ArtOutThere.com
Artoutthere.com has developed a network of artists from across the globe and
believes strongly in supporting the arts in communities worldwide.

ASIAN CULTURAL COUNCIL
Asian Art, Religion, Journalist, Writer Grants--up to $7000
437 Madison Avenue, 37th Floor
New York, NY 10022-7001
(212) 812-4300
http://www.asianculturalcouncil.org
acc@accny.org
The Asian Cultural Council is a foundation determined to support a cultural
exchange between the arts and artisans of the United States and Asia. Grants
are made to individuals pursuing studies in the arts from Asian countries in the
United States and also to United States citizens pursuing artistic studies in Asian
countries.

ASIAN CULTURAL COUNCIL
Japan/United States Artist Grants--up to unknown amt.
437 Madison Avenue, 37th Floor
New York, NY 10022-7001
(212) 812-4300
http://www.asianculturalcouncil.org
acc@accny.org
The Asian Cultural Council is a foundation determined to support a cultural
exchange between the arts and artisans of the United States and Asia. Grants
are made to individuals pursuing studies in the arts from Asian countries in the
United States and also to United States citizens pursuing artistic studies in Asian
countries.

ASIAN CULTURAL COUNCIL
John D. Rockefeller Grant--up to $25,000
437 Madison Avenue, 37th Floor
New York, NY 10022-7001
(212) 812-4300
http://www.asianculturalcouncil.org
acc@accny.org
The Asian Cultural Council is a foundation determined to support a cultural
exchange between the arts and artisans of the United States and Asia. Grants
are made to individuals pursuing studies in the arts from Asian countries in the
United States and also to United States citizens pursuing artistic studies in Asian
countries.

ASIAN CULTURAL COUNCIL
Starr Foundation Grant--up to $15,000+
437 Madison Avenue, 37th Floor
New York, NY 10022-7001
(212) 812-4300
http://www.asianculturalcouncil.org
acc@accny.org
The Asian Cultural Council is a foundation determined to support a cultural
exchange between the arts and artisans of the United States and Asia. Grants
are made to individuals pursuing studies in the arts from Asian countries in the
United States and also to United States citizens pursuing artistic studies in Asian
countries.

ASIAN CULTURAL COUNCIL
Taiwan Artist Grants--up to $20,000
437 Madison Avenue, 37th Floor
New York, NY 10022-7001
(212) 812-4300
http://www.asianculturalcouncil.org
acc@accny.org
The Asian Cultural Council is a foundation determined to support a cultural
exchange between the arts and artisans of the United States and Asia. Grants
are made to individuals pursuing studies in the arts from Asian countries in the
United States and also to United States citizens pursuing artistic studies in Asian
countries.

ASTRAEA LESBIAN FOUNDATION FOR JUSTICE
Artist Grants--up to $2500
116 East 16th Street, 7th Floor
New York, NY 10003
(212) 529-8021
http://www.astraea.org
info@astraea.org
The Astraea Lesbian Foundation for Justice today is the largest lesbian
foundation in the world, providing support to individuals based on the belief that
all women can participate in the philanthropic process-from giving to grant-
making. The foundation supports principles such as feminism, racial and
economic justice, and human rights.

BALTIMORE CLAYWORKS
Lormina Salter Fellowship
5707 Smith Avenue
Baltimore, MD 21209
(410) 578-1919
http://www.baltimoreclayworks.org
leigh.mickelson@baltimoreclayworks.org
Baltimore Clayworks is a non-profit ceramic arts organization that helps to develop, sustain, and promote the work of ceramic artists. This organization hold various educational classes, exhibits artists work, and has other various collaborative programs in the ceramic arts. The Lormina Salter Fellowship is a one year in residence fellowship including stipends and gallery opportunities.

BRITISH SCHOOL IN ROME
Abbey Fellowships in Painting--up to unknown amt.
Via Gramsci 61
Rome,   00197
Italy
00-39-63264939
http://www.bsr.ac.uk
janereid@carson43.demon.co.uk
The British School in Rome is a research institute sponsored by the British Academy in Rome, and serves the interests of fine artists and scholars from the United Kingdom and the United States. Topics of focus at the school include archaeology, history, culture, contemporary art, and architecture. The Abbey Fellowships in Painting include a three month residency and various stipends.

BUHL FOUNDATION
Photography Grants--up to $10,000
114 Greene Street
New York, NY 10012
(212) 274-0100
(Contact by Phone or Mail)
The Buhl Foundation is a private foundation founded in 1927 and awards monetary and other support to individuals not only exploring new ideas in the fine arts, but also many other areas of study including science. Please send a self-addressed stamped envelope and cover letter to the Buhl Foundation for more information and for an application concerning there theme-based photography grant opportunities.

CAROLINE AND ERWIN SWANN FOUNDATION
Artist Grants & Fellowships--up to $15,000
Prints & Photographs Division, Library of Congress
101 Independence Avenue, S.E.
Washington, DC 20540-4730
(202) 707-9115
http://lcweb.loc.gov/rr/print/swann/swannhome.html
swann@loc.gov
The Caroline and Erwin Swann Foundation is a private foundation that is now
administered by the library of congress. The foundations artistic focus is primarily
in the areas of caricature and cartooning.

CARVING STUDIO AND SCULPTURE CENTER
Work Exchange Grants--up to unknown amount
P.O. Box 495
West Rutland, VT 05777
(802) 438-2097
http://www.carvingstudio.org
carving@vermontel.net
The Carving Studio and Sculpture Center is a non-profit organization focused on
assisting artists with the creation of new work in the area of sculpture. Financial
aid in the form of work exchange grants and/or full-fellowships are available to
those who wish to study at the Carving Studio and Sculpture Center.

CEC ARTSLINK
ArtsLink Project Grants--up to $10,000
12 West 31st Street, Suite 400
New York, NY 10001-4415
(212) 643-1985
http://www.cecip.org
cecny@cecip.org
CEC Artslink is an international arts organization and supports collaborative work
between artists from the United States and various countries in Central Europe,
Russia, and Eurasia.

CENTER FOR DOCUMENTARY STUDIES
Dorothea Lange and Paul Taylor Grant--up to $20,000
1317 West Pettigrew Street
Durham, NC 27707
(919) 660-3663
http://cds.aas.duke.edu
docstudies@duke.edu
The Center for Documentary Studies located at Duke University educates, informs, and promotes collaborative works in the areas of photography, film, and documentary writing. The Dorothea Lange and Paul Taylor Grant is awarded to an individual photographer and documentary writer each year who are in the early stages of a collaborative project representing the human story.

CHANGE, INC.
Emergency Artist Grant--up to $500
P.O. Box 54
Captiva, FL 33924
(212) 473-3742
(Call for More Information)
Change, Inc. provides emergency grants to artists in time of need for medical, living, and various other expenses that may cause the artist undue hardship and may affect his/her ability to utilize his/her artistic talents.

CHARLES A. AND ANNE MORROW LINDBERGH FOUNDATION
Artist Grants--up to $10,580
2150 Third Avenue North, Suite 310
Anoka, MN 55303-2200
(763) 576-1596
http://www.lindberghfoundation.org
info@lindberghfoundation.org
The Charles A. and Anne Morrow Lindbergh Foundation is a private foundation that grants monetary support to artists whose art supports the balance between the natural world and modern technology.

CHRISTOPHER COLUMBUS FELLOWSHIP FOUNDATION
Frank Annunzio Award Grants--up to $50,000
110 Genesee Street, Suite 390
Auburn, NY 13021
(315) 258-0090
http://www.columbusfdn.org
judithmscolumbus@cs.com
The Christopher Columbus Fellowship Foundation is an independent Federal Government Agency established to "encourage and support research, study and labor designed to produce new discoveries in all fields of endeavor for the benefit of mankind," an individual seeking monetary support should have a visionary idea or concept that would sustain the legacy of Christopher Columbus.

CRAFT EMERGENCY RELIEF FUND
Emergency Craft Artist Grants--up to $1000
P.O. Box 838
Montpelier, VT 05601-0838
(802) 229-2306
http://www.craftemergency.org
info@craftemergency.org
The Craft Emergency Relief Fund is a non-profit organization and provides direct
monetary and educational support to craft artists in times of need or emergency.
The organization strives to strengthen and support craft artists across the United
States.

CREATIVE CAPITAL FOUNDATION
Artist Grants--up to $20,000
65 Bleecker Street, 7th Floor
New York, NY 10012
(212) 598-9900
http://www.creative-capital.org
info@creative-capital.org
The Creative Capital Foundation is a non-profit organization supporting the
needs of individual artists across the United States. The Creative Capital
Foundation funds artists in the disciplines of visual arts, media arts, performing
arts, and in other various emerging fields of art.

DAIRY BARN CULTURAL ARTS CENTER
Bead Intl. Juried Exhibit Award--up to $1000
8000 Dairy Lane
Athens, OH 45701
(740) 592-4981
http://www.dairybarn.org
artsinfo@dairybarn.org
The Dairy Barn Cultural Arts Center is located in Ohio and supports art and craft
artists whose work represents the cultural heritage of the Ohio Valley region.

DAIRY BARN CULTURAL ARTS CENTER
Quilt Natl. Juried Exhibit Award--up to $1500
8000 Dairy Lane
Athens, OH 45701
(740) 592-4981
http://www.dairybarn.org
artsinfo@dairybarn.org
The Dairy Barn Cultural Arts Center is located in Ohio and supports art and craft
artists whose work represents the cultural heritage of the Ohio Valley region.

DC COMMISSION ON THE ARTS AND HUMANITIES
Multiple Artist Grant Programs--up to $5,000
410 8th Street NW, 5th Floor
Washington, DC 20004
(202) 724-5613
http://dcarts.dc.gov
dcart@dc.gov
The DC Commission on the Arts and Humanities provides monetary support to
individual artists and nonprofit organizations. The DC Commission on the Arts
and Humanities has a variety of grant funding available, please visit their website
for constant updates concerning grant opportunities.

Deutsche Börse Group
The Photography Prize--up to $54,600
The Photographers Gallery
5 Great Newport Street
WC2
London
United Kingdom
http://www.photonet.org.uk/programme/citibank.html
info@photonet.org.uk
The Photographers Gallery, through the Photography Prize Award, seeks to
support the work of a photographer annually whose work raises an awareness of
contemporary photography nationally and internationally. The Deutsche Börse
Group is the primary sponsor and funding partner of the prestigious annual
Photography Prize.

ED FOUNDATION
Artist Grants—up to $5000
953 5th Avenue
New York, NY 10021
(Contact By Mail Only)
The Ed Foundation is a private foundation supporting artists from a variety of
disciplines. Contact should initially be made with a cover letter and self-
addressed stamped envelope in order to receive more information concerning
grants offered by the foundation.

ELIZABETH FOUNDATION FOR THE ARTS
Artist Grants--up to $12,000
P.O. Box 2670
New York, NY 10108
(212) 563-5855
http://www.efacenter.org
grants@efa1.org
The Elizabeth Foundation for the Arts is a private non-profit foundation dedicated
to supporting the needs of individual artists in the United States and abroad.

ELIZABETH GREENSHEILDS FOUNDATION
Artist Grants–up to $10,000
1814 Sherbrooke St.
Montreal, Quebec
Canada, H3H 1E4
(514)937-9225
http://www.calarts.edu/~stdafrs/web/greenshields.html
The Elizabeth Greensheilds Foundation is a foundation dedicated to the educational and monetary support of artists whose work falls into the disciplines of painting, drawing, printmaking, and sculpture.

ELLA LYMAN CABOT TRUST
Artist Grants--up to $20,000
109 Rockland Street
Holliston, MA. 01746
(Contact by Mail)
The Ella Lyman Cabot Trust provides grants to individual artists for specific projects in or outside the artist's field of discipline. Projects must be unique to each individual and provide a good to society.

ERNA AND VICTOR HASSELBLAD FOUNDATION
Stipends and Grants in Photography--up to $10,000
Ekmansgatan 8
SE-412 56 Goteborg
Sweden
46-31-778-1990
http://www.hasselbladfoundation.org
info@hasselbladfoundation.org
The Erna and Victor Hasselblad Foundation is an international private not-for-profit foundation providing monetary support primarily to artists and those in the field of natural sciences. They provide grants for individuals in these fields in the form of grants, research grants, scholarships, stipends, and donations.

FIFTYCROWS FOUNDATION
Grants for Documentary Photography--up to $7,000
1074 Folsom Street
San Francisco, CA 94103
(415) 551-0091
http://www.fiftycrows.org
info@fiftycrows.org
The FiftyCrows Foundation is a non-profit organization providing monetary support to documentary photographers whose work focuses on positive social change.

FINLANDIA FOUNDATION® NATIONAL
Finlandia Foundation Trust Grant--up to $5,000
P.O. Box 832006
Richardson, TX 75083-2006
http://www.finlandiafoundation.org/
secretary@finlandiafoundation.org
The Finlandia Foundation National is a private foundation focused on supporting
individuals and organizations that promote and preserve Finnish culture in the
United States.

FRANCIS GREENBURGER FOUNDATION
Greenburger Artist Grants for Sculptors & Painters--up to $6,000
Executive Director
George Hofmann
55 5th Avenue
New York, NY 10003
(212) 206-6092
(Contact By Phone or Mail)
The Francis Greenburger Foundation is a foundation providing monetary support
to artists in the fields of painting and sculpting. Please contact the foundation at
their mailing address and include a self-addressed stamped envelope for specific
information regarding their grant programs.

GEORGE A. AND ELIZA GARDNER HOWARD FOUNDATION
Fellowship Grants--up to $20,000
Brown University
Box 1867
Providence, RI 02912
(401) 863-2640
http://www.brown.edu/Divisions/Graduate_School/howard/
Howard_Foundation@brown.edu
The George and Eliza Gardner Howard Foundation is a private foundation
providing monetary support to individuals in the arts and social sciences. The
fellowships offered by the foundation are primarily geared towards mid-career
artists and individuals in the fields of social science whose work is
representational of their lifetime career achievements.

GEORGE SUGARMAN FOUNDATION
Artist Grants--up to $10,000
448 Ignacio Blvd., #329
Novato, CA 94949
(415) 713-8167
http://www.georgesugarman.com
ardensugarman@hotmail.com
The George Sugarman Foundation is a private foundation focused on providing
monetary support to young and/or emerging artists in multiple fields of discipline.

GREELEY ART COMMISSION
Sculpture on Loan Program--up to $500
Cultural Affairs Office
651 10th Ave.
Greeley, CO 80631
(970) 350-9454
http://www.ci.greeley.co.us/
rosentrj@ci.greeley.co.us
The Greeley Art Commission is a city-based commission started in 1995. The commission selects sculpture artists whose work will be put on public display annually.

GREENWICH HOUSE POTTERY
Artist Grant/Scholarship--up to unknown amt.
16 Jones Street
New York, NY 10014-4132
(212) 242-4106
http://www.greenwichhousepottery.com
pottery@greenwichhouse.org
The Greenwich House Pottery is an organization begun in 1909, and promotes the ceramic arts through education, community gatherings, exhibitions and other events.

GUNK FOUNDATION
Public Art Project Grants--up to $5,000
P.O. Box 333
Gardiner, NY 12525
(845) 255-8252
http://www.gunk.org
info@gunk.org
The Gunk Foundation is a private charitable foundation established in 1994. The Gunk Foundation primarily supports public art projects, especially non-traditional projects.

INSTITUTE OF INTERNATIONAL EDUCATION
Cintas Fellowship Grants--up to $10,000
809 United Nations Plaza
New York, NY 10017-3580
(212) 883-8200
http://www.iie.org
info@iie.org
The Institute of International Education was founded in 1919. The Cintas Fellowship is limited to practicing artists with Cuban citizenship or direct Cuban lineage.

INTERNATIONAL CENTER OF PHOTOGRAPHY
W. Eugene Smith Grant in Humanistic Photography--up to $35,000
1114 Avenue of the Americas
New York, NY 10036
(212) 857-0000
http://www.icp.org
http://www.smithfund.org
education@icp.org
The International Center of Photography is an organization encompassing a
museum, educational opportunities, and other assistance for photographers.

J. PAUL GETTY TRUST
Getty Scholar Grants--up to $75,000
1200 Getty Center Drive
Los Angeles, CA 90049-1681
(310) 440-7300
http://www.getty.edu
info@getty.edu
The J. Paul Getty Trust is an international cultural and philanthropic organization
dedicated to supporting artists from all genres. The trust was begun in 1953 and
strives to promote artistic education nationwide.

JINGDEZHEN SANBAO CERAMIC ART INSTITUTE
Fellowship Program-Ceramics
14 Courtwright Road
Etobicoke
Toronto, M9C4B4
CANADA
(416) 695-3607
http://www.chinaclayart.com
chinaxchange@hotmail.com
Jingdezhen Sanbao Ceramic Art Institute is an organization that strives to
promote the ceramic arts on an international level.

JOHN SIMON GUGGENHEIM MEMORIAL FOUNDATION
Guggenheim Fellowships--up to $36,000
90 Park Ave.
New York, NY 10016
(212) 687-4470
http://www.gf.org/
fellowships@gf.org
The John Simon Guggenheim Memorial Foundation was established in 1925 by
United States Senator Simon Guggenheim and primarily supports artists
monetarily in various fields of research.

KATE NEAL KINLEY MEMORIAL FELLOWSHIP
Artist Fellowship Award up to--$15,000
608 E. Lorado Taft Dr.
Champaign, IL 61820
(217) 333-1661
(Contact by Phone or Mail)
The Kate Neal Kinley Memorial Fellowship is fellowship program providing monetary support to artists.

LEICA INTERNATIONAL PHOTOGRAPHIC COMPETITION
Photographer Grants up to --$5,000
Oskar-Barnack-Straße 11
D-35606
Solms
Germany
4906442-208-0
http://www.leica-camera.com
info@leica-camera.com
Leica Internationals Oskar Barnack Award was established in 1979. Oskar Barnack was noted for developing the world's first 35mm camera. Leica is a German based company which produces a multitude of products for the photography industry.

LIQUITEX ART MATERIAL AWARDS
Artist Material Awards up to--$5000
11 Church Lane
P.O. Box 1396
Piscataway, NJ 08855
(888) 422-7954
http://www.liquitex.com
The Liquitex Corporation is an established business providing reliable and affordable top quality artist materials to artisans of all genres.

LUDWIG VOGELSTEIN FOUNDATION
Artist Grants up to--$5,000
P.O. Box 510
Shelter Island, NY 11964-0510
Contact by Mail with (SASE) included
The Ludwig Vogelstein Foundation is a foundation which provides monetary support to artists.

NATIONAL SCULPTURE SOCIETY
Artist Grants up to--$4000
The Park Avenue Atrium
237 Park Avenue
New York, NY 10017
(212) 764-5645
http://www.nationalsculpture.org
The National Sculpture Society is an organization founded in 1893. The National Sculpture Society awards annually the Alex J. Ettl Grant to a realist sculptor.

NORTH AMERICAN NATURE PHOTOGRAPHY ASSOCIATION
Artist Grants up to--$1,000
10200 West 44th Avenue, Suite 304
Wheat Ridge, CO 80033-2840
(303) 422-8527
http://www.nanpa.org
info@nanpa.org
The North American Nature Photography Association was founded in 1998. The association awards the Janie Moore Green Grant to a qualified student in the field of photography annually.

THE NORTH AMERICAN REVIEW
Artist Competition Award up to--$300
University of Northern Iowa
1222 W. 27th Street
Cedar Falls, IA 50614
http://webdelsol.com/NorthAmReview/NAR
nar@uni.edu
The University of Northern Iowa is a collegiate institution.

PHOTO REVIEW
Artist Award up to--$250
140 East Richardson Ave., Suite 301
Langhorne, PA 19047-2824
(215) 891-0214
http://www.photoreview.org
info@photoreview.org
The Photo Review is a print publication promoting the art of photography.

POLLOCK-KRASNER FOUNDATION
Artist Grants up to--$unknown amt.
863 Park Avenue
New York, NY 10021
(212) 517-5400
http://www.pkf.org
grants@pkf.org
The Pollock-Krasner Foundation is a private foundation, was begun in 1985, and provides monetary support to visual artists internationally.

PUFFIN FOUNDATION
Artist Grants up to--$2,500
Dept. B, 20 East Oakdene Avenue
Teaneck, NJ 07666-4198
(201) 836-8923
http://www.puffinfoundation.org/
puffingrant@mindspring.com
The Puffin Foundation is a private foundation that was established in 1983. The foundation strives to promote the work of artists who come from non-traditional or underprivileged backgrounds.

SCHOOL OF AMERICAN RESEARCH
Artist Grants up to--$unknown amt.
PO Box 2188
Santa Fe, NM 87504-2188
(505) 954-7200
http://www.sarweb.org
iarc@sarsf.org
The School of American Research is a non profit institutional center for advanced studies and monetarily supports working artists; the school was founded in 1907.

SILVER EYE CENTER FOR PHOTOGRAPHY
Photographer Grants up to--$2,000
1015 East Carson Street
Pittsburgh, PA 15203
(412) 431-1810
http://www.silvereye.org
silvereyegallery@aol.com
The Silver Eye Center for Photography is an organization dedicated to promoting photography as a powerful art form. The center was founded in 1984.

SOCIETY FOR CONTEMPORARY CRAFT
Artist Grants up to--$5,000
2100 Smallman Street
Pittsburgh, PA 15222
(412) 261-7003
http://www.contemporarycraft.org
info@contemporarycraft.org
The Society for Contemporary Craft, founded in 1997, is an organization that promotes contemporary arts and crafts by providing guidance and monetary support to artisans.

U.S. - MEXICO FUND FOR CULTURE
Artist Grants up to--$30,000
Londres 16, 3er Piso
Col. Juarez, D.F., 06600
Mexico
525-592-53-86
http://www.fidemexusa.org.mx
info@culturalcontact.org
The U.S. – Mexico Fund for Culture is an organization striving to preserve and promote the arts and culture of both Mexico and the United States.

URSULA BLICKLE FOUNDATION
Artist Grants up to--$10,000
Mühlweg 18, D-76703
Kraichtal-Unteröwisheim,
Germany
(+49) 725160919
http://www.ursula-blickle-stiftung.de
office@ursula-blickle-stiftung.de
The Ursula Blickle Foundation is private foundation, established in 1991, and strives to promote traditional and non-traditional contemporary art forms.

VIRGINIA A. GROOT FOUNDATION
Ceramic Artist Grants--up to $35,000
P.O. Box 1050
Evanston, IL 60204-1050
(763) 550-9003
(Write for More Info. with SASE)
The Virginia A. Groot Foundation is a private foundation that provides monetary support to ceramic and sculpture artisans.

WOMEN'S STUDIO WORKSHOP
Artist Book Production Grants up to--$1,000
P.O. Box 489
722 Binnewater Lane
Rosendale, NY 12472
(845) 658-9133
http://www.wsworkshop.org
wsw@ulster.net
The Women's Studio Workshop is an organization that provides monetary
support to female artists seeking to complete and publish a book or other
publication.

WORLDSTUDIO FOUNDATION
Artist Scholarships up to--$5,000
225 Varick St. 9th Fl.
New York, NY 10014
(212) 366-1317
http://www.worldstudio.org
rstikeman@hotmail.com
The Worldstudio Foundation is a private not for profit foundation, was established
in 1993, and strives to promote diversity in the arts by providing monetary
support to young artists in the form of scholarships amongst other forms of aid.

Western USA Grants and Fellowships

ARTIST TRUST
Artist Grants--up to $1400
1835 12th Avenue
Seattle , WA 98122
(206) 467-8734
http://www.artisttrust.org
info@artisttrust.org
Artist trust is a not-for-profit organization dedicated to supporting individual
Washington State artisans including musicians, writers, visual and craft artists,
playwrights, choreographers, composers, performers and filmmakers.

ARTIST TRUST
Washington State Arts Commission Grant--up to $6000
1835 12th Avenue
Seattle, WA 98122
(206) 467-8734
http://www.artisttrust.org
info@artisttrust.org
(WA. Residency Req.)
Artist trust is a not-for-profit organization dedicated to supporting individual
Washington State artisans including musicians, writers, visual and craft artists,
playwrights, choreographers, composers, performers and filmmakers.

ARTIST TRUST
Twining Humber Award for Lifetime Artistic Achievement—up to $10,000
1835 12th Avenue
Seattle, WA 98122
(206) 467-8734
http://www.artisttrust.org
info@artisttrust.org
(WA. Residency Req.)
Artist trust is a not-for-profit organization dedicated to supporting individual
Washington State artisans including musicians, writers, visual and craft artists,
playwrights, choreographers, composers, performers and filmmakers.

CALIFORNIA COMMUNITY FOUNDATION
Artist Grants--up to $15,000
445 S. Figueroa Street, Suite 3400
Los Angeles, CA 90071-1638
(213) 413-4130
http://www.calfund.org
aparachi@ccf-la.org
(CA. Residency Req.)
The California Community Foundation is a non-profit foundation and provides
monetary support to organizations and or individuals that foster cultural
awareness and promote the humanities.

CALIFORNIA COUNCIL FOR THE HUMANITIES
California Documentary Grant--up to $20,000
312 Sutter Street, Suite 601
San Francisco, CA 94108
(415) 391-1474
http://www.calhum.org
info@calhum.org
(CA. Residency Req.)
The California Council for the Humanities is a non-profit organization and
provides monetary support to organizations and or individuals that foster cultural
awareness and promote the humanities.

CITY OF ALBUQUERQUE PUBLIC ART PROGRAM
Artist Grants--up to $20,000
P.O. Box 1293
Albuquerque, NM 87103
(505) 768-3829
http://www.cabq.gov/publicart/
aescher@cabq.gov
(NM. Residency Req.)
The City of Albuquerque Public Art Program is administered by the city of
Albuquerque, New Mexico, and provides monetary funds for art projects city-
wide.

CITY OF BOULDER ARTS COMMISSION
Artists Grants--up to $5,000
Boulder Arts Resource
Boulder Public Library
P.O. Drawer H
Boulder, CO 80306
(303) 441-4113
http://artist.bldr.net/BAC.cfm
(CO. Residency Req.)
The City of Boulder Arts Commission is administered by the city of Boulder,
Colorado, and was established to foster an increased awareness in the arts.

CREATIVE WORK FUND
Artist Grants--up to $35,000
One Lombard Street, Suite 305
San Francisco, CA 94111-1130
(415) 398-4474
http://www.creativeworkfund.org
jean@haassr.org
(CA. Residency Req.)
The Creative Work Fund is a non-profit organization that fosters relations and
provides monetary support for individual artists and other non-profit organizations
to collaborate on art projects.

CULTURAL ARTS COUNCIL OF HOUSTON AND HARRIS COUNTY
Artist Grants--up to $2500
3201 Allen Parkway, 2nd Floor
Houston, TX 77019-1800
(713) 527-9330
http://www.cachh.org
info@cachh.org
(TX. Residency Req.)
The Cultural Arts Council of Houston and Harris County is a non-profit
organization that seeks to foster relations between artisans and the communities
of Houston and Harris County through communicatory and monetary support.

DALLAS MUSEUM OF ART
Arch and Anne Giles Kimbrough Grant--up to $3,500
Department of Contemporary Art
1717 North Harwood Street
Dallas, TX 75201
(214) 922-1200
http://www.dm-art.org
(TX. Residency Req.)
The Dallas Museum of Art was established in 1903 and strives to promote and support the fine arts locally, nationally, and internationally.

DALLAS MUSEUM OF ART
Clare Hart Degolyer Memorial Grant--up to $1,500
Department of Contemporary Art
1717 North Harwood Street
Dallas, TX 75201
(214) 922-1200
http://www.dm-art.org
(AR., CO., NM., OK., TX. Residency Req.)
The Dallas Museum of Art was established in 1903 and strives to promote and support the fine arts locally, nationally, and internationally.

DALLAS MUSEUM OF ART
Otis and Velma Davis Dozier Travel Grant--up to $6,000
Department of Contemporary Art
1717 North Harwood Street
Dallas, TX 75201
(214) 922-1200
http://www.dm-art.org
(TX. Residency Req.)
The Dallas Museum of Art was established in 1903 and strives to promote and support the fine arts locally, nationally, and internationally.

DURFEE FOUNDATION
Artists' Resource for Completion—up to $2500
1453 Third Street, Suite 312
Santa Monica, CA 90401
(310) 899-5120
http://www.durfee.org
admin@durfee.org
(CA. Residency Req.)
The Durfee Foundation is a private foundation that strives to support artisans and art organizations.

FLINTRIDGE FOUNDATION
Artist Grants--up to $25,000
1040 Lincoln Avenue, Suite 100
Pasadena, CA 91103
(626) 449-0839
http://www.flintridgefoundation.org
FFAVA@FlintridgeFoundation.org
(CA., OR., WA. Residency Req.)
The Flintridge Foundation is a non-profit foundation that strives to monetarily
support individuals and or groups in the fine arts.

SERPENT SOURCE FOUNDATION FOR WOMEN ARTISTS
Artist Grants up to--$2,300
3311 Mission Street, #176
San Francisco, CA 94110
(415) 597-3545
http://home.flash.net/~serpents
SerpSource@aol.com
(CA. Residency Req.)
The Serpent Source Foundation for Women Artists is a non-profit foundation
established to provide encompassing support to women artisans.

Midwestern USA Grants and Fellowships

ARROWHEAD REGIONAL ARTS COUNCIL
Artist Grants--up to $4500
1301 Rice Lake Road
Suite 111
Duluth, MN 55811
(800) 569-8134
http://www.aracouncil.org/
ARACouncil@aol.com
(MN. Residency Req.)
The Arrowhead Regional Arts Council strives to promote, support, and
encourage the development of artisans.

ARROWHEAD REGIONAL ARTS COUNCIL
Artist Grants--up to $1000
1301 Rice Lake Road
Suite 111
Duluth, MN 55811
(800) 569-8134
http://www.aracouncil.org/
ARACouncil@aol.com
(MN. Residency Req.)
The Arrowhead Regional Arts Council strives to promote, support, and
encourage the development of artisans.

ARROWMONT SCHOOL OF ARTS AND CRAFTS
East Tennessee Woodworkers Guild Grant--up to $500
P.O. Box 567
556 Parkway
Gatlinburg, TN 37738-0567
(865) 436-5860
http://www.arrowmont.org
info@arrowmont.org
(TN. Residency Req.)
The Arrowmont School of Arts and Crafts is an educational centre where artist's
can practice and develop their chosen artistic goals.

ARTSERVE MICHIGAN
Artist Grants--up to $8000
17515 West Nine Mile Road, Suite 1025
Southfield, MI 48075
(248) 557-8288
http://www.artservemichigan.org
info@artservemichigan.org
(MI. Residency Req.)
Artserve Michigan is an organization that strives to support, promote, and encourage the development of the arts in their communities.

BUSH FOUNDATION
Bush Artist Grant--$40,000+
332 Minnesota Street
East 900
St. Paul, MN 55101
(651) 227-0891
info@bushfoundation.org
(MN, SD, ND, WI Residency Req.)
The Bush foundation strives to promote and encourage learning and development in the fine arts.

CENTRAL MINNESOTA ARTS BOARD
Artist Awards--up to $2750
P.O. Box 750
Elk River, MN 55330
(763) 241-9517
mail@cmab.org
(MN. Residency Req.)
The Central Minnesota Arts Board strives to promote and encourage learning and development in the fine arts.

CHICAGO ARTISTS' COALITION
Ruth Talaber Artist Emergency Grants--up to $500
11 East Hubbard, 7th Floor
Chicago, IL 60611
(312) 670-2060
http://www.caconline.org
cacwebmaster@caconline.org
(IL. Residency Req.)

CULTURE WORKS
Artist Grants & Fellowships--up to $10,000
126 North Main Street, Suite 210
Dayton, OH 45402
(937) 222-2787
http://www.cultureworks.org
pattyrosely@cultureworks.org
(OH. Residency Req.)
Culture Works is an organization that promotes cultural and artistic development
throughout the Dayton, Ohio area.

DANE COUNTY CULTURAL AFFAIRS COMMISSION
Artist Grants--up to $10,000
City-County Building, Room 42,
210 Martin Luther King Jr. Boulevard
Madison, WI 53709
(608) 266-5915
http://www.co.dane.wi.us/dcca/index.html
cultural.affairs@co.dane.wi.us
(WI. Residency Req.)
The Dane County Cultural Affairs Commission strives to monetarily support and
in other ways promote artistic culture.

FIGGE MUSEUM OF ART
Brand Boeshaar Scholarships--up to $3,000
1737 West 12th Street
Davenport, IA 52804
(563) 326-7804
http://www.art-dma.org
amh@ci.davenport.ia.us
(IA., IL. Residency Req.)
The Figge Museum of Art strives to promote and support the fine arts and
provides a scholarship to 4 graduating high school seniors each year.

FIVE WINGS ART COUNCIL
Artist Grants--up to $500
200 First Street NE
Staples, MN 56479
(218) 894-5485
http://www.fwac.org
mturner@ncscmn.org
(MN. Residency Req.)
The Five Wings Art Council is an organization that promotes cultural and artistic
development throughout qualified areas of Minnesota via monetary and other
developmental support.

GATEWAY FOUNDATION
Great River Biennial Visual Art Grants--up to $15,000
720 Olive Street, Suite 1977
Saint Louis, MO 63101
(314) 241-3337
http://www.gateway-foundation.org
gwf1977@aol.com
(MO. Residency Req.)
The Gateway Foundation strives to promote and encourage learning and
development in the fine arts through monetary and other support.

GREATER COLUMBUS ARTS COUNCIL, INC.
Fellowship Program
55 East State Street 6th Floor
Columbus, OH 43215
(614) 224-2606
http://www.gcac.org
info@gcac.org
The Greater Columbus Arts Council, Inc. strives to promote and encourage
learning and development in the fine arts through monetary and other support.

JEROME FOUNDATION
Artist Grants--up to $25,000
125 Park Square Court, 400 Sibley Street
St. Paul, MN 55101-1928
(651) 224-9431
http://www.jeromefdn.org
info@jeromefdn.org
(MN., NY. Residency Req.)
The Jerome Foundation strives to promote and encourage learning and
development in the fine arts through monetary and other support of individual
artists.

NORTHERN CLAY CENTER
Artist Grants up to--$6,000
2424 Franklin Ave. E
Minneapolis, MN 55406
(612) 339-8007
http://www.northernclaycenter.org
(MN. Residency Req.)
The Northern Clay Center strives to promote and encourage learning and
development in the ceramic arts.

OKLAHOMA VISUAL ARTS COALITION
Artist Fellowship Grants up to--$5,000
P.O. Box 54416
Oklahoma City, OK 73154
http://www.ovac-ok.org
director@ovac-ok.org
(OK. Residency Req.)
The Oklahoma Visual Arts Coalition strives to promote and encourage learning and development in the fine arts.

Eastern USA Grants and Fellowships

ARLINGTON COUNTY CULTURAL AFFAIRS DIVISION
Arlington Commission for the Arts Grant--up to $10,000
3700 S. Four Mile Run Drive
Arlington, VA 22206-2304
(703) 228-1850
http://www.arlingtonarts.org
arts@co.arlington.va.us
(VA. Residency Req.)
The Arlington County Cultural Affairs Division's artist grants provide monetary
and or other support to practicing artists and arts organizations.

ARTISTS SPACE
Artist Grant--up to $500
38 Greene Street, 3rd floor
New York, NY 10013
(212) 226-3970
http://www.artistsspace.org
artspace@artistsspace.org
(NY. Residency Req.)
The Artist's Space is a non-profit arts organization, and is one of these first
alternative art spaces in New York. The organization strives to promote diversity
and growth in the arts through monetary and other support of artisans.

BALTIMORE OFFICE OF PROMOTION AND THE ARTS
Community Art Grants--up to $3000
7 East Redwood Street, Suite 500
Baltimore, MD 21202
(410) 752-8632
http://www.promotionandarts.com
gkachadourian@promotionandarts.com
(MD. Residency Req.)
The Baltimore Office of Promotion and the Arts strives to support the arts and
fine arts through monetary and other support throughout the Baltimore areas.

BERKSHIRE TACONIC COMMUNITY FOUNDATION
Artist Grants--up to $10,000
271 Main Street–Suite 3
Great Barrington, MA 01230
(800) 969-2823
http://www.berkshiretaconic.org
info@berkshiretaconic.org
(MA. Residency Req.)
The Berkshire Taconic Community Foundation strives to support the arts through monetary and other support to individuals and groups in the Berkshire Taconic region.

CASWELL COUNCIL FOR THE ARTS
Artist Grant--up to $2500
PO Box 689
Yanceyville, NC 27379-0689
(336) 694-4591
www.uacgreensboro.org
ccfta@vnet.net
(NC. Residency Req.)
The Caswell Council for the Arts grant provides monetary and other support to practicing artists and arts organizations in the region.

CINTAS FOUNDATION
Oscar B. Cintas Foundation Fellowship--up to $10,000
Institute of International Education
809 United Nations Plaza
New York, NY 10017-3580
(212) 984-5565
http://www.iie.org/programs/fulbright/cintas/
cintas@iie.org
(NY. Residency Req.)
The Cintas Foundation Fellowship provides monetary support to practicing artists with Cuban lineage, but not currently residing in Cuba.

CITY OF ATLANTA, BUREAU OF CULTURAL AFFAIRS
Artist Grant--up to $1000
675 Ponce de Leon Avenue, NE, 5th Floor
Atlanta, GA 30308
(404) 817-6815
http://www.ci.atlanta.ga.us/citydir/prca/cultural/cultural.htm
bca@ci.atlanta.ga.us
(GA. Residency Req.)
The Bureau of Cultural Affairs of the City of Atlanta provides monetary and other support to practicing artists and arts organizations in the region.

CONSTANCE SALTONSTALL FOUNDATION FOR THE ARTS
Individual Artist Grants—up to $5000
435 Ellis Hollow Creek Road
Ithaca, NY 14850
(607) 539-3146
http://www.saltonstall.org/
info@saltonstall.org
(NY. Residency Req.)
The Constance Saltonstall Foundation for the Arts grant provides monetary and
other support to practicing artists and arts organizations in the region.

CULTURAL COUNCIL OF GREATER JACKSONVILLE
Art Education Grants--up to $500
300 West Water Street, Suite 201
Jacksonville, FL 32202
(904) 358-3600
http://www.culturalcouncil.org
info@culturalcouncil.org
(FL. Residency Req.)
The Cultural Council of Greater Jacksonville art education grant provides
monetary support to artists in the region.

FRANZ AND VIRGINIA BADER FUND
Artist Grants--up to $25,000
5505 Connecticut Avenue, NW #268
Washington, DC 20015-2601
(202) 288-4608
http://www.baderfund.org
grants@baderfund.org
(DC. Residency Req.)
The Cultural Council of Greater Jacksonville art education grant provides
monetary support to artists in the region.

GARRISON ART CENTER
SOS Artist Grant—up to $600
P.O. Box 4
23 Garrison's Landing
Garrison, NY 10524
(845) 424-3960
http://www.garrisonartcenter.org
dir@garrisonartcenter.org
The Garrison Art Center grant provides monetary support to artists in the region.

PEW ARTIST FELLOWSHIPS
Artist Grants up to--$50,000
The University of the Arts
230 South Broad Street, Suite 1003
Philadelphia, PA 19102
(215) 875-2285
http://www.pewarts.org
pewarts@mindspring.com
(PA. Residency Req.)
The PEW Artist Fellowship provides monetary support to artisans.

WORKING FUND FOR PHILADELPHIA AREA ARTISTS LIVING WITH
HIV/AIDS
Artist Grants up to--$unknown amt.
Samuel S. Fleisher Art Memorial
709-721 Catharine Street
Philadelphia, PA 19147
(215) 922-3456
http://www.critpath.org/workfund/workfund.htm
workfund@critpath.org
(PA. Residency Req.)
The Working Fund for Philadelphia Area Artists Living with HIV/AIDS strives to
promote and assist artisans affected by this illness.

Chapter 3

Residency Programs for Artists

AIR-VALLAURIS ASSOCIATION
Residence Program
Place Lisnard
1 Boulevard des Deux Vallons
Vallauris,   06220
France
http://air-vallauris.com
contact@air-vallauris.com

ANDERSON RANCH ARTS CENTER
Residence Program
P.O. Box 5598
5263 Owl Creek Road
Snowmass Village, CO 81615
(970) 923-3181
http://www.andersonranch.org
info@andersonranch.org

APPALACHIAN CENTER FOR CRAFTS
Residence Program
1560 Craft Center Drive
Smithville, TN 37166
(615) 597-6801
http://www.craftcenter.tntech.edu
craftcenter@tntech.edu

ARCHIE BRAY FOUNDATION FOR THE CERAMIC ARTS
Bill & Stirling Sage Scholarship/Residency/Fellowship Programs
2915 Country Club Avenue
Helena, MT 59602
(406) 443-3502
http://www.archiebray.org
archiebray@archiebray.org

ART FARM
Artist Colony/Residence Program
1306 West 21st Road
Marquette, NE 68854-2112
(402) 854-3120
--No Website Available--
Housing and Studio Access Provided
artfarm@hamilton.net

ARTPARK
Residence Program
450 South Fourth Street
Lewiston, NY 14092
(716) 754-9000
http://www.artpark.net
boffice@artpark.net

BANFF CENTRE FOR THE ARTS
Visual Arts Residencies
Office of the Registrar
Box 1020, Stn. 28
107 Tunnel Mt. Drive
Banff, Alberta, Canada
(403)762-6180

BODANNA, INC.
Residence Program-Ceramics
125 East 7th Street
New York, NY 10009
(212) 388-0078
http://www.bodanna.org
thelma@bodanna.org

CENTER FOR DOCUMENTARY STUDIES
CDS/Honickman First Book Prize Competition--up to $3000
1317 West Pettigrew Street
Durham, NC 27707
(919) 660-3663
http://cds.aas.duke.edu
docstudies@duke.edu

CHESTER SPRINGS STUDIO
Residence Program
1671 Art School Road
P.O. Box 329
Chester Springs, PA 19425
(610) 827-7277
http://www.chesterspringsstudio.org
csstudio@chesterspringsstudio.org

CLAY ART CENTER
Residence Program
40 Beech Street
Port Chester, NY 10573
(914) 937-2047
http://www.clayartcenter.org
mail@clayartcenter.org

CLAY STUDIO
Residence/Fellowship Program
139 North 2nd Street
Philadelphia, PA 19106
(215) 925-3453
http://www.theclaystudio.org
info@theclaystudio.org

CONTEMPORARY CRAFTS ASSOCIATION
Residence Program-Ceramics
3934 SW Corbett Avenue
Portland, OR 97201
(503) 223-2654
--No Website Available--
--Write for More Info.--
Stipend and Studio Space

THE HELENE WURLITZER FOUNDATION
Residence Program
The Helene Wurlitzer Foundation of New Mexico
P.O. Box 545
Taos, NM.

HENRY STREET SETTLEMENT
Residence Program-Ceramics
Abrons Art Center
466 Grand Street
New York, NY 10002-4804
(212) 598-0400
http://www.henrystreet.org
info@henrystreet.org

JALOM ARTIST RESIDENCY PROGRAM
Residence Program - Visual Arts, Writing, Music
Jalom Artist Residency Program
Attn: Marietta Bernstorff, Coordinator
Callejon, Amapola #7
Barrio Cuxtitali, San Cristobal de las Casas
Chiapas, Mexico 29230

JOHN MICHAEL KOHLER ARTS CENTER
Residence Program-Ceramics
608 New York Avenue, P.O. Box 489
Sheboygan, WI 53082-0489
(920) 458-6144
http://www.jmkac.org

LAKESIDE STUDIO
Residence Program-Ceramics
600 North McClurg Court
Suite 1302-A
Chicago, IL 60611
--Write for More Info.--

LIGHT WORK
Residence Program-Photography
Light Work
316 Waverly Avenue
Syracuse, NY. 13244
(315)443-2450

MCCOLL CENTER FOR THE VISUAL ARTS
Residence Program
721 North Tryon Street
Charlotte, NC 28202
(704) 332-5535
http://www.mccollcenter.org/

MORAVIAN POTTERY AND TILE WORKS
Apprenticeship Program
130 Swamp Road
Doylestown, PA 18901
(215) 345-6722
http://www.buckscounty.org/departments/tileworks
moravianpotteryandtileworks@co.bucks.pa.us

NEWARK MUSEUM
Residence Program
49 Washington Street
Box 540
Newark, NJ 07101
(973) 596-6550
http://www.newarkmuseum.org

NOTTINGHAM CENTER FOR THE ARTS
Residence Program
PO Box 460
San Marcos, CA 92079
(760) 752-1020
http://www.nottinghamarts.org
registrar@nottinghamarts.org

OREGON COLLEGE OF ARTS AND CRAFTS
Residence Program
8245 SW Barnes Road
Portland, OR 97225
(800) 390-0632
http://www.ocac.edu

PALM BEACH COUNTY CULTURAL COUNCIL
Residence Program
1555 Palm Beach Lakes Boulevard #300
West Palm Beach , FL 33401
(561) 471-2901
http://www.pbccc.org

PENLAND SCHOOL OF CRAFTS
Residence Program
P.O. Box 37
Penland, NC 28765-0037
(828) 765-2359
http://www.penland.org
office@penland.org

PETERS VALLEY CRAFT EDUCATION CENTER
Residence/Assistant Program
19 Kuhn Road
Layton, NJ 07851
(973) 948-5200
http://www.pvcrafts.org
pv@warwick.net

PEWABIC POTTERY
Residence Program
10125 East Jefferson Avenue
Detroit, MI 48214
(313) 822-0954
http://www.pewabic.com
pewabic1@pewabic.com

WATERSHED CENTER FOR THE CERAMIC ARTS
Residence Program
19 Brick Hill Road
Newcastle, ME 04553
(207) 882-6075
http://www.watershedcenterceramicarts.org
h2oshed@midcoast.com

WORCESTER CENTER FOR CRAFTS
Residence Program
25 Sagamore Road
Worcester, MA 01605
(508) 753-8183
http://www.worcestercraftcenter.org/
wcc@worcestercraftcenter.org

Chapter 4

Major Art and Craft Galleries and Retailers

Abacus
44 Exchange Street
Portland, ME. 4101
207-772-4880

Accipiter
2046 Clark Avenue
Raleigh, NC. 27605
919-755-9309

Agora Arts
104 East Water Street #1
Decorah, Iowa 52101
563-382-8786

A Mano Gallery
128 South Main Street
New Hope, PA. 18938
215-862-5122

American Artisan
4231 Harding Road
Nashville, TN. 37205
615-298-4691

American Craft Gallery
163 South Street
Morristown, NJ. 7960
973-538-6720

An American Craftsman
1866 Route 284
P.O. Box 480
Slate Hill
New York, NY. 10973
845-355-2400

Annapolis Pottery
40 State Circle
Annapolis, MD. 21401
410-268-6153

Art Craft Collection
8600 Foundry Street
Savage, MD. 20763
410-880-4863

Artful Hand Gallery
36 Copley Place
Boston, MA. 2116
617-262-9601

Artique
161 Lexington Green Circle
Lexington, KY. 40503
859-272-8802

Artisan Center
2757 East 3rd Avenue
Denver, CO. 80206
303-333-1201

Artisan's Gallery
Box 133
Shop #35
Peddler's Village
Lahaska, PA. 18931
215-794-3112

Arts and Artisans Ltd.
36 South Wabash
Suite #604
Chicago, IL. 60603
312-855-9220

Arts Company
125 North Townville Street
Seneca, SC. 29678
864-882-0840

Bluestem Missouri Crafts
13 South Ninth Street
Colombia, MO. 65201
573-442-0211

Browning Artworks Ltd.
Highway 12
P.O. Box 275
Frisco, NC. 27936-0275
252-995-5538

Cambridge Artist Cooperative
59A Church Street
Cambridge, MA. 2138
617-868-5966

Campbell Pottery Store
25579 Plank Road
P.O. Box 246
Cambridge Springs, PA. 16403
814-734-8800

Capitol Craftsman
16 North Main Street
Concord, NH. 3301
603-224-6166

CBL Fine Art
459 Pleasant Valley Way
West Orange, NJ. 7052
973-736-7776

Citywoods
651 Central Avenue
Highland Park, IL. 60035
847-432-9393

Clarksville Pottery Galleries
4001 N Lamar Boulevard
Central Market, #200
Austin, TX. 78756
512-454-8930

Clay Pot
162 7th Avenue
Brooklyn, NY. 11215
718-788-6564

Craft Company No. 6
785 University Avenue
Rochester, NY. 14607
716-473-3413

Creations Fine Woodworking Gallery
451 Hockessin Corner
Hockessin, DE. 19707
302-235-2310

Dennison-Moran Gallery
696 5th Avenue South
Naples, FL. 34102
941-263-0590

Designer's Studio
492 Broadway
Saratoga Springs, NY. 12866
518-584-1977

Dickinson and Wait Craft Gallery
121 East German Street
P.O. Box 1273
Shepherdstown, WV. 25443
304-876-0657

Don Muller Gallery
40 Main Street
Northampton, MA. 1060
413-586-1119

Dream Weaver
364 St. Armands Circle
Sarasota, FL. 34236
941-388-1974

Dunn Mehler Gallery
337 Mirada Road
Half Moon Bay, CA. 94019
650-726-7667

Earthenworks Gallery
713 First Street
P.O. Box 702
La Conner, WA. 98257
360-466-4422

Edgecomb Potters Galleries
727 Boothbay Road
Edgecomb, ME. 4556
207-882-9493

Edgewood Orchard Galleries
4140 Peninsula Player Road
Fish Creek, WI. 54212
920-868-3579

Evergreen Contemporary Crafts
291 Main Street
Great Barrington, MA. 1230
413-528-0511

Fabrile Gallery
224 South Michigan Avenue
Chicago, IL. 60604
312-427-1510

Fireworks Gallery
210 First Avenue South
Seattle, WA. 98104
206-682-8707

Freehand Fine Crafts
8413 West Third Street
Los Angeles, CA. 90048
323-655-2607

Gallery 3-2-1
65 West State Street
P.O. Box 369
Oxford, NY. 13830
607-843-9538

Gallery of the Mountains
290 Macon Avenue
P.O. Box 8283
Asheville, NC. 28804
828-254-2068

Glass Reunions of Key West
825 Duval Street
Key West, FL. 33040
305-294-1720

Good Goods Gallery
106 Mason Street
Saugatuck, MI. 49453
616-857-1557

Grovewood Gallery
111 Grovewood Road
Asheville, NC. 28804
828-253-7651

Handworks Gallery
161 Great Road
Acton, MA. 1720
978-263-1707

Hanson Galleries
800 West Sam Houston Parkway North
#E118
Houston, TX. 77024
713-984-1242

Heart to Heart Gallery
921 Ridge Road
Munster, IN. 46321
219-836-2300

Island Style
2075 Periwinkle
#16
Sanibel Island, FL. 33957
941-472-6657

Kebanu
4-1354 Kuhio
Highway #3
Kapaa Kauai, HI. 96746
808-823-6820

Lazar's Art Gallery
2940 Woodlawn Avenue NW
Canton, OH. 44708
330-477-8351

Left Bank Gallery
25 Commercial Street
P.O. Box 764
Wellfleet, MA. 2667
508-349-9451

Limited Editions
2200 Long Beach Boulevard
Surf City, NJ. 8008
609-494-0527

Log House Craft Gallery
Berea College
Berea, KY. 40404
859-985-3226

Luma
1 Lake Avenue
P.O. Box 1439
Colorado Springs, CO. 80901
719-577-5853

Mackerel Sky Gallery
217 Ann Street
East Lansing, MI. 48823
517-351-2211

Mind's Eye Craft Gallery
201 South Talbot Street
P.O. Box 781
St. Michaels, MD. 21663
410-745-2023

Moondance Gallery
603 Meadowmont Village Circle
Chapel Hill, NC. 27517
919-726-0020

Mostly Clay and Fine Crafts
227 Broad Street
Nevada City, CA. 95959
530-265-3535

Mountain Laurel Crafts
1 North Washington Street
P.O. Box 369
Berkeley Springs, WV. 25411
304-258-1919

Nancy Markoe Fine American Crafts Gallery
3112 Pass A Grille Way
St. Pete Beach, FL. 33706
727-360-0729

NJM Gallery
8 Bow Street
Portsmouth, NH. 3801
603-433-4120

Patina Gallery
131 West Palace Avenue
Santa Fe, NM. 87501
505-986-3432

Pismo Gallery
235 Fillmore Street
Denver, CO. 80206
303-333-2879

Primavera
4 Bowen's Wharf
Newport, RI 2840
401-841-0757

Purple Sage
110 Don Gaspar
Santa Fe, NM. 87501
505-984-0600

RAF
5 West York Street
Savannah, GA. 31401
912-447-8807

Raiford Gallery
1169 Canton Street
Roswell, GA. 30075
770-645-2050

Raspberry's Art Glass Gallery
6540 Washington Street
Yountville, CA. 94599
707-944-9211

Sansar
4805 Bethesda Avenue
Bethesda, MD. 20814
301-652-8676

Seekers Glass Gallery
4090 Burton Drive
P.O. Box 521
Cambria, CA. 93428
805-927-8626

Selo/Shevel Gallery
301 South Main Street
Ann Arbor, MI. 48104
734-761-4620

Shapiro's
185 Second Avenue North
St. Petersburg, FL. 33701-0714
727-894-2111

Signature Stores
10 Steeple Street
P.O. Box 2307
Mashpee, MA. 2649
508-539-0029

Snyderman Works Gallery
303 Cherry Street
Philadelphia, PA. 19106
215-922-7775

Society of Arts and Crafts
175 Newbury Street
Boston, MA. 2116
617-266-1810

Stone's Throw Gallery
1389 Beacon Street
Brookline, MA. 2146
617-731-3773

Stowe Craft Gallery
55 Mountain Road
Stowe, VT. 5672
802-253-4693

Studio 41
700 First Street
Benicia, CA. 94510
707-745-0254

Suprises
4003 Westheimer
Houston, TX. 77027
713-877-1900

Topeo Gallery
35 North Main Street
New Hope, PA. 18938
215-862-2750

Vault
1339 Pacific Avenue
Santa Cruz, CA. 95060
831-426-3349

Village Artisans Gallery
321 Walnut Street
P.O. Box 303
Boiling Springs, PA. 17007
717-258-3256

Chapter 5

Specialty Art Book Publishers

A and C Black
37 Soho Square
London
W1D 3QZ
Telephone: 0207 758 0200
http://www.acblack.com/
A UK based publisher, located in London, founded in 1807, specializing in
ornithology, travel, arts and crafts, who's who, nautical, performing arts,
children's, art writing, music, ceramics and glass, sports, and reference
publishing genres.

Abbeville Press
116 W. 23rd Street
Suite 500
New York, New York 10011
Phone: (646) 375-2039
Fax: (646) 375-2040
http://www.abbeville.com/
A New York based publisher, located in New York City, founded in 1977,
specializing in art and illustrated books. As of April, 2004 Abbeville is no longer
accepting unsolicited submissions.

Actar Publishers
Roca i Batlle 2
08023 Barcelona
Tel +34 93 418 77 59
Fax +34 93 418 67 07
info@actar-mail.com
www.actar.es
A publisher based in Barcelona, Spain, specializing in art, architecture, design,
photography publishing.

Afton Historical Society Press
PO Box 100
Afton, MN 55001
Fax: 1-651-436-7354
Phone: 1-800-436-8443
Local Calls 1-651-436-8443
aftonpress@aftonpress.com
http://www.aftonpress.com/
(Online Manuscript Submission Available)
A non-profit historical publisher based in Afton, Minnesota, specializing in art and
architecture, history, photography, native, and gardening publishing.

Allworth Press
10 East 23rd Street
Suite 210
New York, NY, 10010
http://www.allworth.com/
(Online Manuscript Submission Available)
Publishes on a wide range of art topics from general art, photography, and
performing arts, to self-help and graphic design related books.

Amherst Media
P.O. Box 586
Amherst, NY. 14226
716-874-4450
www.amherstmedia.com
A New York based publisher, specializing in art and photography publishing.

Architectural Press
Elsevier Science/Harcourt
200 Wheeler Road
6th floor
Burlington MA 01803, USA
Telephone: 781-221-2212
Fax: 781-221-1615
usbkinfo@elsevier.com
http://www.bh.com/architecturalpress/
(Online Manuscript Submission Available)
An international publisher, located in Massachusetts, specializing in art and
architecture publishing.

Arnoldsche Art Publishers
ARNOLDSCHE Verlagsanstalt GmbH
Liststraße 9
D-70180 Stuttgart
Telefon +49/711/64 56 18 0
Fax +49/711/64 56 18 79
USA -- ACC Ltd.
Telefon +1/845/2 97 00 03
Fax +1/845/2 97 00 68
http://www.arnoldsche.com/
An international German based publisher, with offices world-wide, specializing in
arts and crafts, photography, ceramics, interior, jewelry, design, and other misc.
publishing.

Balcony Press
512 East Wilson
Suite 213
Glendale California 91206
818 956-5313
818 956-5904 fax
contact@balconypress.com
(Online Manuscript Submission Available)
http://www.balconypress.com/index.html
A California based publisher, founded in 1994, specializing in art, architecture,
and design publishing.

Bayeux Arts, Inc.
119 Stratton Crescent S.W.
Calgary, Alberta
T3H 1T7, CANADA
V: (403) 249-2477
F: (403) 249-2477
calgary@bayeux.com
A Canadian based publisher, specializing in art, architecture, literature, and
children's publishing.

Bright Ring Publishing, Inc.
P.O. Box 31338
Bellingham, WA 98228-3338
1-800-480-4278
submissions@brightring.com
A Washington based publisher, specializing in children's publishing.

Brown Trout Publishers, Inc.
P.O. Box 280070
San Francisco, CA 94128-0070
310.316.4480
800.777.7812
production@browntrout.com
http://www.browntrout.com/
A California based publisher, founded in 1986, specializing in fine art
photography publishing. Please visit their website for specific image submission
guidelines.

Chronicle Books, LLC.
85 Second Street, Sixth Floor
San Francisco, California 94105
Tel: 415-537-4200 or 800-722-6657
Fax: 415-537-4460
frontdesk@chroniclebooks.com
http://www.chroniclebooks.com/Chronicle/servlet/at/info
A California based publisher, founded in 1966, specializing in art, architecture, photography, children's, and misc. publishing.

Counterpoint Press
Acquisitions Editor
Basic Books
387 Park Ave. South
New York, NY 10016
http://www.counterpointpress.com/contact.html
A New York based publisher, specializing in serious literary works in the arts, history, poetry, fiction, science, philosophy, and other misc. topics.

David Porteous Editions
P.O. Box 5,
Chudleigh
Newton Abbot
Devon, TQ13 0YZ, England
editorial@davidporteous.com
http://www.davidporteous.com/
A U.K. based publisher, specializing in arts and crafts books.

Davis Publications
Davis Publications, Inc
50 Portland St.
Worcester, MA 01608
1 (800) 533-2847
http://www.davis-art.com/
A U.S. based publisher located in Massachusettes, leading in the publication of art education books.

Howell Press, Inc.
1713-2D Allied Lane,
Charlottesville, Virginia 22903 USA
Phone (800)868-4512
Fax (888)971-7204
custserv@howellpress.com
http://www.howellpress.com/
A Charlottesville, Virginia based publisher, specializing in art, photography, history, cooking/food, and other misc. publishing.

Long Wind Publishing
c/o Publisher
PO Box 13024
Fort Pierce, FL, 34979
publisher@longwindpub.com
http://www.longwindpub.com/contact.asp
A Fort Pierce, Florida publisher, specializing in art, photography, and mystery
publishing.

Mainstream Publishing
7 Albany Street
Edinburgh EH1 3UG
Tel: 0131 557 2959
Fax: 0131 556 8720
enquiries@mainstreampublishing.com
http://www.mainstreampublishing.com/contact.html
Publisher based in Edinburgh, specializing in art, photography, sports, current
affairs, and other misc. topics.

The Overlook Press
Attn: The Editors
The Overlook Press
141 Wooster Street
New York, NY 10012
http://www.overlookpress.com/contact.php
A New York based publisher, specializing in art and general publishing, please
visit their website for specific manuscript submission information.

Chapter 6

Poster and Print Publishers

Anabas Fine Arts, LTD.
P.O. Box 754
Brentwood
Essex CM145TR
United Kingdom
44-1277-372222
kim@anabas.co.uk
www.anabasonline.com
Publishes posters.

Art In Motion
2000 Hartley Avenue
Coquitlam
British Columbia
V3K 6W5
Canada
604-525-3900
artdirector@artinmotion.com
www.artinmotion.com
Publishes prints and posters.

The Art Publishing Group
Artist Submissions
276 Fifth Avenue- Suite 205
New York, New York 10001
submitart@theartpublishinggroup.com
www.theartpublishinggroup.com
Publishes prints and posters.

Bentley Publishing Group
1410 Lesnick Lane
Walnut Creek, CA. 94596
925-935-3186
info@bentleypublishinggroup.com
www.bentleypublishinggroup.com
Publishes posters.

Bon Art/Art Resources INT. LTD.
281 Fields Lane
Brewster, NY. 10509
845-277-8888
robin@fineartpublishers.com
www.fineartpublishers.com
Publishes prints and posters.

Deljou Art Group
1616 Huber Street
Atlanta, GA. 30318
404-350-7190
mail@deljouartgroup.com
www.deljouartgroup.com
Publishes prints.

Dina Art Comapny
6433 Sunset Blvd
Los Angeles, CA. 90028
Attn. Dina Goldstein
www.dinaart.com
Publishes prints and posters.

Directional Publishing, Inc.
Attn: Art Selection Committee
2812 Commerce Square East
Birmingham, AL 35210
artdirector@dp1.net
www.directionalart.com
Publishes prints and posters.

Finger Hut Group Publishers, Inc.
800-525-7456
rann@fingerhutart.com
http://www.fingerhutart.com/
Publishes prints and posters.

Fotofolio, INC.
561 Broadway
New York, NY. 10012
212-226-0923
submissions@fotofolio.com
www.fotofolio.com
Publishes posters.

Front Line Art Publishing
5897 Oberlin Drive
Suite 211
San Diego, CA. 92121
858-552-0944
submitart@theartpublishinggroup.com
www.frontlineartpublishing.com
Publishes prints and posters.

Gango Editions
351 NW 12th
Portland, OR. 97034
503-223-9694
jackie@gangoeditions.com
www.gangoeditions.com
Publishes prints.

Island Art
P.O. BOX 22063
Brentwood Bay, BC, V8M 1R5
Canada
1-800-663-7501
www.islandart.com
Publishes prints and posters.

Modern Art
276 5th Avenue
Suite 205
New York, NY. 10001
212-779-0700
marymize@aol.com
www.modernarteditions.com
Publishes prints and posters.

New Era Fine Art Publishing
Attn: Art Review
2101 E. St. Elmo Rd. Suite 110.
Austin, TX 78744
888-928-3910
http://www.newerapublishing.com/Index.asp
Publishes prints and posters.

Nors Graphics
P.O. Box 143
Woolwich, ME. 04579
207-442-0159
nors@loa.com
www.norsgear.com
Publishes prints and posters.

Penny Lane Publishing
Attn: Artist Coordinator
1791 Dalton Drive
New Carlisle, OH 45344
http://www.pennylanepublishing.com/html/Home.html
Publishes prints and posters.

Portfolio Graphics, INC.
P.O. Box 17437
Salt Lake City, UT. 84117
801-266-4844
info@portfoliographics.com
www.portfoliographics.com
Publishes prints and posters.

Posters International
Attn: Artist Submissions
1200 Castlefield Avenue
Toronto, Ontario
M6B 1G2 Canada
800-363-2787
art@postersinternational.net
http://www.postersinternational.net/index.php
Publishes prints and posters.

Rosenstiel's Fine Art Publishing
33-35 Markham Street
London SW3 3NR
United Kingdom
www.felixr.com/information
Publishes prints.

Wild Apple Graphics
Wild Apple Licensing
526 Woodstock Road
Woodstock, VT. 05091
902-457-3003
www.wildapple.com
licensing@wildapple.com
Publishes prints.

INDEX OF OPPORTUNITIES

National and International Grants and Fellowships

A ROOM OF HER OWN FOUNDATION
AARON SISKIND FOUNDATION
ADOLPH AND ESTHER GOTTLIEB FOUNDATION
AID FOR ARTISANS, INC.
ALDRICH MUSEUM OF CONTEMPORARY ART
ALEXIA FOUNDATION
ALLIANCE FOR YOUNG ARTISTS & WRITERS
ALLIGATOR JUNIPER
AMERICAN CERAMIC CIRCLE, INC.
AMERICAN INSTITUTE OF ARCHITECTS
AMERICAN WATERCOLOR SOCIETY
ART LIBRARIES SOCIETY OF NORTH AMERICA
ARTADIA
ARTIST TRUST
ARTISTS' FELLOWSHIP
ARTOUTTHERE.COM
ASIAN CULTURAL COUNCIL
ASTRAEA NATIONAL LESBIAN ACTION FOUNDATION
BALTIMORE CLAYWORKS
BRITISH SCHOOL IN ROME
BUHL FOUNDATION
CAROLINE AND ERWIN SWANN FOUNDATION
CARVING STUDIO AND SCULPTURE CENTER
CEC ARTSLINK
CENTER FOR DOCUMENTARY STUDIES
CHANGE, INC.
CHARLES A. AND ANNE MORROW LINDBERGH FOUNDATION
CHRISTOPHER COLUMBUS FELLOWSHIP FOUNDATION
CITIGROUP PRIVATE BANK
CRAFT EMERGENCY RELIEF FUND
CREATIVE CAPITAL FOUNDATION
DAIRY BARN CULTURAL ARTS CENTER
DC COMMISSION ON THE ARTS AND HUMANITIES
ED FOUNDATION
ELIZABETH FOUNDATION FOR THE ARTS
ELIZABETH GREENSHEILDS FOUNDATION
ELLA LYMAN CABOT TRUST
ERNA AND VICTOR HASSELBLAD FOUNDATION
FIFTYCROWS FOUNDATION
FINLANDIA FOUNDATION® NATIONAL
FRANCIS GREENBURGER FOUNDATION
GEORGE A. AND ELIZA GARDNER HOWARD FOUNDATION

GEORGE SUGARMAN FOUNDATION
GREATER COLUMBUS ARTS COUNCIL, INC.
GREELEY ART COMMISSION
GREENWICH HOUSE POTTERY
GUNK FOUNDATION
INDIAN ARTIST DISASTER RELIEF FUND
INSTITUTE OF INTERNATIONAL EDUCATION
INTERNATIONAL CENTER OF PHOTOGRAPHY
J. PAUL GETTY TRUST
JINGDEZHEN SANBAO CERAMIC ART INSTITUTE
JOAN MITCHELL FOUNDATION
JOHN SIMON GUGGENHEIM MEMORIAL FOUNDATION
KATE NEAL KINLEY MEMORIAL FELLOWSHIP
LEF FOUNDATION
LEICA INTERNATIONAL PHOTOGRAPHIC COMPETITION
LIQUITEX ART MATERIAL AWARDS
LUDWIG VOGELSTEIN FOUNDATION
NATIONAL SCULPTURE SOCIETY
NORTH AMERICAN NATURE PHOTOGRAPHY ASSOCIATION
THE NORTH AMERICAN REVIEW
PHOTO REVIEW
POLLOCK-KRASNER FOUNDATION
PUFFIN FOUNDATION
SCHOOL OF AMERICAN RESEARCH
SILVER EYE CENTER FOR PHOTOGRAPHY
SOCIETY FOR CONTEMPORARY CRAFT
SOHO PHOTO GALLERY
U.S. - MEXICO FUND FOR CULTURE
URSULA BLICKLE FOUNDATION
VIRGINIA A. GROOT FOUNDATION
WOMEN'S STUDIO WORKSHOP
WORLDSTUDIO FOUNDATION

Western USA Grants and Fellowships

ALASKA STATE COUNCIL ON THE ARTS
ARIZONA COMMISSION ON THE ARTS
ARTIST TRUST
CALIFORNIA COMMUNITY FOUNDATION
CALIFORNIA COUNCIL FOR THE HUMANITIES
CITY OF ALBUQUERQUE PUBLIC ART PROGRAM
CITY OF BOULDER ARTS COMMISSION
COLORADO COUNCIL ON THE ARTS
CREATIVE WORK FUND
CULTURAL ARTS COUNCIL OF HOUSTON AND HARRIS COUNTY
CULTURAL DEVELOPMENT AUTHORITY OF KING COUNTY

MUSEUM OF ART
DURFEE FOUNDATION
FLINTRIDGE FOUNDATION
NEVADA ARTS COUNCIL
SERPENT SOURCE FOUNDATION FOR WOMEN ARTISTS
UTAH ARTS COUNCIL
WASHINGTON STATE ARTS COMMISSION
WYOMING ARTS COUNCIL

Midwestern USA Grants and Fellowships

ALABAMA STATE COUNCIL ON THE ARTS
ARKANSAS ARTS COUNCIL
ARROWHEAD REGIONAL ARTS COUNCIL
ARROWMONT SCHOOL OF ARTS AND CRAFTS
ARTSERVE MICHIGAN
BUSH FOUNDATION
CHICAGO ARTISTS' COALITION
CULTURE WORKS
DANE COUNTY CULTURAL AFFAIRS COMMISSION
DAVENPORT MUSEUM OF ART
FIVE WINGS ART COUNCIL
ILLINOIS ARTS COUNCIL
JEROME FOUNDATION
KANSAS ARTS COMMISSION
MISSISSIPPI ARTS COMMISSION
NEBRASKA ARTS COUNCIL
NORTHERN CLAY CENTER
OHIO ARTS COUNCIL
OKLAHOMA VISUAL ARTS COALITION
SOUTH DAKOTA ARTS COUNCIL
TENNESSEE ARTS COMMISSION

Eastern USA Grants and Fellowships

ARLINGTON COUNTY CULTURAL AFFAIRS DIVISION
ARTISTS SPACE
BALTIMORE OFFICE OF PROMOTION AND THE ARTS
BERKSHIRE TACONIC COMMUNITY FOUNDATION
CASWELL COUNCIL FOR THE ARTS
CINTAS FOUNDATION
CITY OF ATLANTA, BUREAU OF CULTURAL AFFAIRS
CONNECTICUT COMMISSION ON THE ARTS
CONSTANCE SALTONSTALL FOUNDATION FOR THE ARTS
CULTURAL COUNCIL OF GREATER JACKSONVILLE
DELAWARE DIVISION OF THE ARTS

FRANZ AND VIRGINIA BADER FUND
GARRISON ART CENTER
MAINE ARTS COMMISSION
NEW HAMPSHIRE STATE COUNCIL ON THE ARTS
NEW JERSEY STATE COUNCIL ON THE ARTS
NEW YORK STATE COUNCIL ON THE ARTS
NORTH CAROLINA ARTS COUNCIL
PENNSYLVANIA COUNCIL ON THE ARTS
PEW ARTIST FELLOWSHIPS
RHODE ISLAND STATE COUNCIL ON THE ARTS
SOUTH CAROLINA ARTS COMMISSION
VIRGIN ISLANDS COUNCIL ON THE ARTS
VIRGINIA COMMISSION FOR THE ARTS
WEST VIRGINIA COMMISSION ON THE ARTS
WORKING FUND FOR PHILADELPHIA AREA ARTISTS LIVING WITH
HIV/AIDS

Residency Programs For Artists

AIR-VALLAURIS ASSOCIATION
ANDERSON RANCH ARTS CENTER
APPALACHIAN CENTER FOR CRAFTS
ARCHIE BRAY FOUNDATION FOR THE CERAMIC ARTS
ART FARM
ARTPARK
BANFF CENTRE FOR THE ARTS
BODANNA, INC.
CENTER FOR DOCUMENTARY STUDIES
CHESTER SPRINGS STUDIO
CLAY ART CENTER
CLAY STUDIO
CONTEMPORARY CRAFTS ASSOCIATION
THE HELENE WURLITZER FOUNDATION
HENRY STREET SETTLEMENT
JALOM ARTIST RESIDENCY PROGRAM
JOHN MICHAEL KOHLER ARTS CENTER
LAKESIDE STUDIO
LIGHT WORK
MCCOLL CENTER FOR THE VISUAL ARTS
MORAVIAN POTTERY AND TILE WORKS
NEWARK MUSEUM
NOTTINGHAM CENTER FOR THE ARTS
OREGON COLLEGE OF ARTS AND CRAFTS
PALM BEACH COUNTY CULTURAL COUNCIL
PENLAND SCHOOL OF CRAFTS
PETERS VALLEY CRAFT EDUCATION CENTER

PEWABIC POTTERY
WATERSHED CENTER FOR THE CERAMIC ARTS
WORCESTER CENTER FOR CRAFTS

Major Art and Craft Galleries and Retailers

Abacus
Accipiter
Agora Arts
A Mano Gallery
American Artisan
American Craft Gallery
An American Craftsman
Annapolis Pottery
Art Craft Collection
Artful Hand Gallery
Artique
Artisan Center
Artisan's Gallery
Arts and Artisans Ltd.
Arts Company
Bluestem Missouri Crafts
Browning Artworks Ltd.
Cambridge Artist Cooperative
Campbell Pottery Store
Capitol Craftsman
CBL Fine Art
Citywoods
Clarksville Pottery Galleries
Clay Pot
Craft Company No. 6
Creations Fine Woodworking Gallery
Dennison-Moran Gallery
Designer's Studio
Dickinson and Wait Craft Gallery
Don Muller Gallery
Dream Weaver
Dunn Mehler Gallery
Earthenworks Gallery
Edgecomb Potters Galleries
Edgewood Orchard Galleries
Evergreen Contemporary Crafts
Fabrile Gallery
Fireworks Gallery
Freehand Fine Crafts
Gallery 3-2-1

Gallery of the Mountains
Glass Reunions of Key West
Good Goods Gallery
Grovewood Gallery
Handworks Gallery
Hanson Galleries
Heart to Heart Gallery
Island Style
Kebanu
Lazar's Art Gallery
Left Bank Gallery
Limited Editions
Log House Craft Gallery
Luma
Mackerel Sky Gallery
Mind's Eye Craft Gallery
Moondance Gallery
Mostly Clay and Fine Crafts
Mountain Laurel Crafts
Nancy Markoe Fine American Crafts Gallery
NJM Gallery
Patina Gallery
Pismo Gallery
Primavera
Purple Sage
RAF
Raiford Gallery
Raspberry's Art Glass Gallery
Sansar
Seekers Glass Gallery
Selo/Shevel Gallery
Shapiro's
Signature Stores
Snyderman Works Gallery
Society of Arts and Crafts
Stone's Throw Gallery
Stowe Craft Gallery
Studio 41
Suprises
Topeo Gallery
Vault
Village Artisans Gallery

Specialty Art Book Publishers

A and C Black

Abbeville Press
Actar Publishers
Afton Historical Society Press
Allworth Press
Amherst Media
Architectural Press
Arnoldsche Art Publishers
Balcony Press
Bayeux Arts, Inc.
Bright Ring Publishing, Inc.
Brown Trout Publishers, Inc.
Chronicle Books, LLC.
Counterpoint Press
David Porteous Editions
Davis Publications
Howell Press, Inc.
Long Wind Publishing
Mainstream Publishing
The Overlook Press

Poster and Print Publishers

Anabas Fine Arts, LTD.
Art In Motion
The Art Publishing Group
Bentley Publishing Group
Bon Art/Art Resources INT. LTD.
Deljou Art Group
Dina Art Comapny
Directional Publishing, Inc.
Finger Hut Group Publishers, Inc.
Fotofolio, INC.
Front Line Art Publishing
Gango Editions
Island Art
Modern Art
New Era Fine Art Publishing
Nors Graphics
Penny Lane Publishing
Portfolio Graphics, INC.
Posters International
Rosenstiel's Fine Art Publishing
Wild Apple Graphics